**Riddles That Rhyme
for Halloween Time**

Riddles That Rhyme for Halloween Time

By Leonard Kessler

GARRARD PUBLISHING COMPANY
CHAMPAIGN, ILLINOIS

Riddles That Rhyme
for Halloween Time

Willa Witch wishes she had
some hair on her head.
What would she buy?

A big wig

Talk louder
I can't
hair you!

6

Willa Witch's kitten
eats a lot.
When it grows up,
what has she got?

7

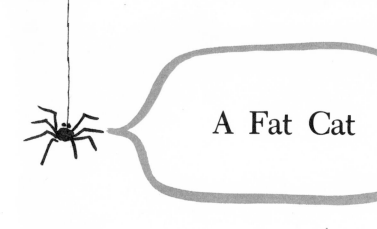

A Fat Cat

Willa Witch's rabbit
lies on the beach all day.
What does she have?

A sunny bunny

What is a sweet rabbit?

A HONEY BUNNY!

Jolly Ghost's silly rabbit
makes Willa Witch laugh a lot.
What has he got?

A funny bunny

Willa Witch puts tuna
in Fat Cat's bowl.
What does he have?

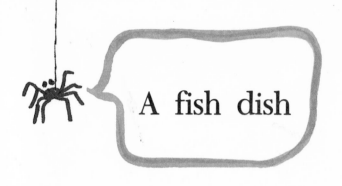

A fish dish

Willa Witch puts magic water
in her pot.
She puts in meat, potatoes,
and carrots.
She stirs it up.
What has she got?

Willa Witch cooks
a spooky story
in her bubbling pot.
What is she?

A book cook!

The Jolly Ghost steals the story
from the bubbling pot.
What is he?

A book crook

Willa Witch has a good mouse.
Jolly Ghost has a good mouse.
What do they have?

Fat Cat chases the mice
into their hole.
Where do the mice live?

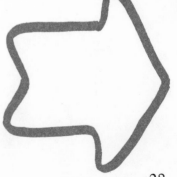

In a mouse house

Willa Witch flies off on her broom.
She lands in poison ivy.
What does she have?

A witch itch

Jolly Ghost is at bat.
Willa throws the ball.
She strikes him out with what?

A witch pitch

Fat Cat chews up
Willa Witch's baseball glove.
What does she have?

A bit mitt

Willa Witch polishes her boots.
What do the boots have?

A fine shine

32

Willa Witch and Jolly Ghost
sing through Halloween night.
They sing and sing.
What are they singing?

A long song

Willa Witch has a runny nose.

She has had it for a long time.

What does she have?

An old cold

Willa's Fat Cat
got caught in the rain.
What does Willa call him?

A wet pet

It's raining on Halloween.

It's wet in Willa's cave.

Her bed is under water.

What does she have?

A sunk bunk

Pickles! Pickles!

For trick or treat.

Five cents each.

Jolly Ghost buys one.

What does he buy?

A nickle pickle

42

Willa Witch's parrot
eats crackers all day.
What does she call him?

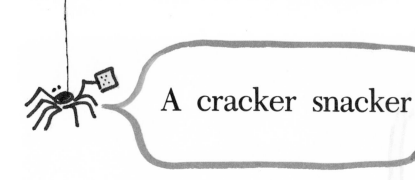

A cracker snacker

Willa Witch sits in the park.
She makes Jolly Ghost
and Fat Cat
put their trash in a can.
What is Willa Witch?

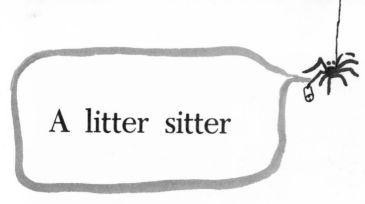

A litter sitter

Fat Cat, Jolly Ghost,
and Willa Witch
had lots of fun
on Halloween night.
What did they have?

A keen Halloween

The answer now is on the door.
Can you think of any more?